THE
Sammy
Davis Jr.
SONGBOOK

Piano
Vocal
Guitar

T0045159

ISBN 0-634-09018-6

HAL•LEONARD®
CORPORATION
7777 W. BLUEMOUND RD. P.O. BOX 13819 MILWAUKEE, WI 53213

Visit Hal Leonard Online at
www.halleonard.com

Biography

The voice is instantly recognized by millions of people around the world, as is the man himself. There is something personal about his presence, which commands attention and respect. His name is Sammy Davis Jr. and he was, without question, the most complete entertainer of his time. He was a singer, dancer, actor, musician, comedian, author and film and television producer. His efforts to aid the underprivileged and ease racial tensions were boundless. He appeared at over sixty benefits a year.

He began as a determined, wide-eyed kid out of Harlem working with his father and his uncle in dingy, low-paying clubs. He was making the big time in a big way—he gave four Royal Command performances in London—when he was badly injured in a car crash and lost his left eye. As soon as he recovered, he went back on stage. His opening night performance at Hollywood's famous Ciro's was a tumultuous triumph, sold out with every major star in attendance.

Davis recorded over 30 LP albums. His many singles have sold more than 15 million copies. Recordings etched with his unmistakable style include "Hey There," "What Kind of Fool Am I?," "Gonna Build A Mountain," "The Shelter of Your Arms" and "I've Gotta Be Me." Sammy's first gold record, "The Candy Man," sold an unbelievable 4 million copies. Davis was instrumental in breaking down racial barriers in film and television. He appeared on every major nationally televised musical show in the '60s and '70s. His film appearances include *Ocean's Eleven*, *Sweet Charity* and *Porgy and Bess*. He performed on Broadway, in the starring role, in *Golden Boy*, which has become a Broadway classic.

Sammy was the first African-American man to own a Las Vegas hotel. He was many times awarded the Las Vegas Entertainer of the Year. "The Sammy Davis Jr. Greater Hartford Open" marked the first time the PGA named a golf tournament for a black man. Sammy formed Alto Records, named after his wife, Altovise Gore Davis. He owned Trans-American Video. He performed in Viet Nam. His more than 500 awards include the Achievement Freedom Award, the Springarm Medal of the NAACP, and the Alan Bernstein Award for cancer research. There are very few places in the world where Davis didn't perform.

In 1990, Davis passed away from throat cancer. His widow, Altovise, keeps his legacy alive with her tireless commitment to the stated mission of the Sammy Davis Jr. Foundation to introduce the fine arts to youth of all social and economic backgrounds throughout the world. The Sammy Davis Jr. Estate, through its business representation, the LaRoda Group, continues to produce events each year that celebrate the legend that was the World's Greatest Entertainer. In 2003, two new biographies were published, and in 2004, a major feature film is in development, several musical revues and tribute performers around the globe bring Sammy's music to live audiences every night, and a new theatrical production, *Mr. Bojangles: The Ultimate Entertainer*, will begin touring casinos across the U.S.

Contents

AS LONG AS SHE NEEDS ME

from the Columbia Pictures - Romulus Motion Picture Production of Lionel Bart's
OLIVER!

Words and Music by
LIONEL BART

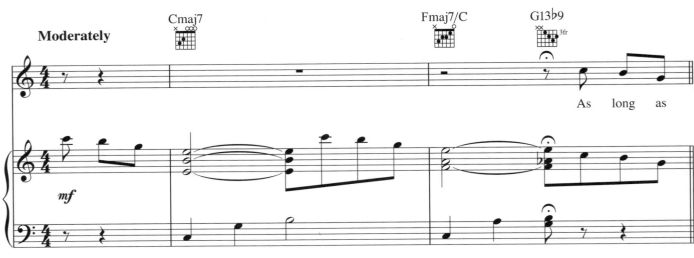

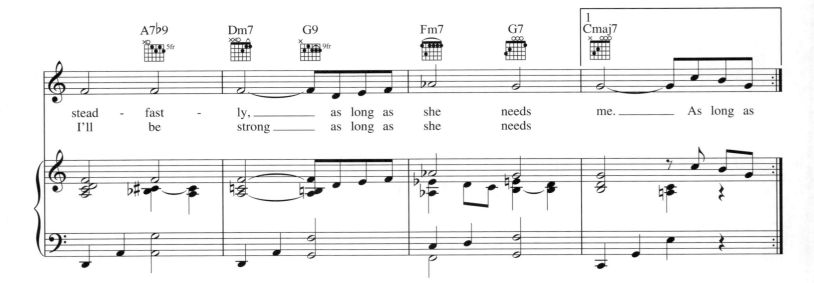

me. _____ If you are lone - ly _____ then you will know _____ when some - one

needs you _____ you love them so. _____ I won't be - tray her

trust, _____ though peo - ple say I must. _____ I've got to

stay true, just _____ as long as she needs me.

THE BIRTH OF THE BLUES

Words by B.G. DeSYLVA and LEW BROWN
Music by RAY HENDERSON

BYE BYE BLACKBIRD

Lyric by MORT DIXON
Music by RAY HENDERSON

THE CANDY MAN
from WILLY WONKA AND THE CHOCOLATE FACTORY

Words and Music by LESLIE BRICUSSE
and ANTHONY NEWLEY

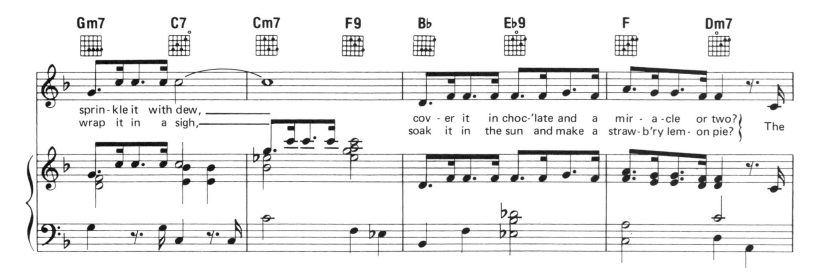

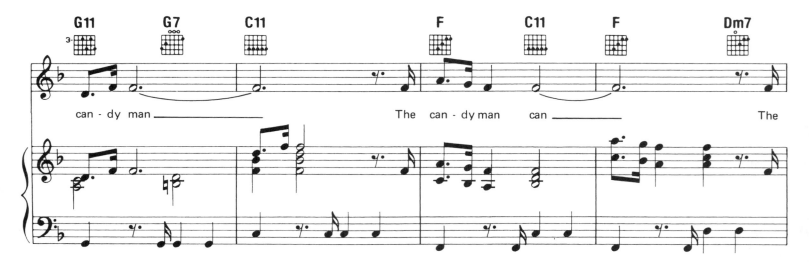

16

I WANT TO BE WITH YOU

from GOLDEN BOY

Lyric by LEE ADAMS
Music by CHARLES STROUSE

GEE BABY, AIN'T I GOOD TO YOU

Words by DON REDMAN and ANDY RAZAF
Music by DON REDMAN

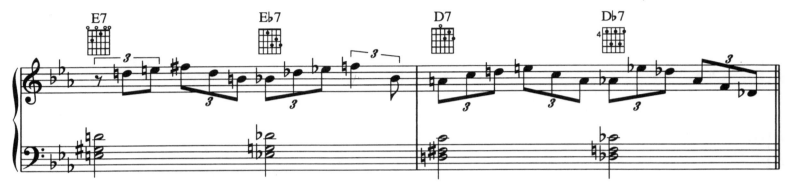

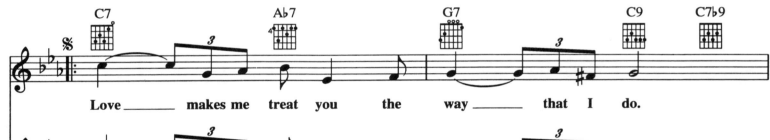

Love _____ makes me treat you the way _____ that I do.

Gee ba-by, ain't I good _ to you! There's noth - in' too good for a

GONNA BUILD A MOUNTAIN

from the Musical Production STOP THE WORLD–I WANT TO GET OFF

Words and Music by LESLIE BRICUSSE
and ANTHONY NEWLEY

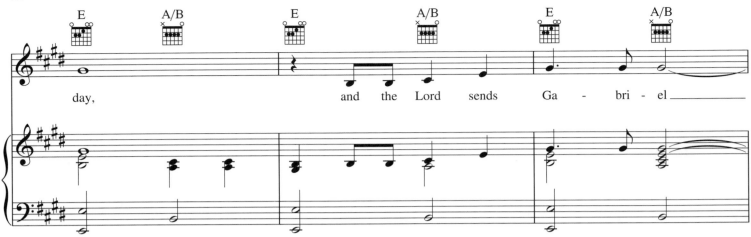

day, and the Lord sends Ga - bri - el ____

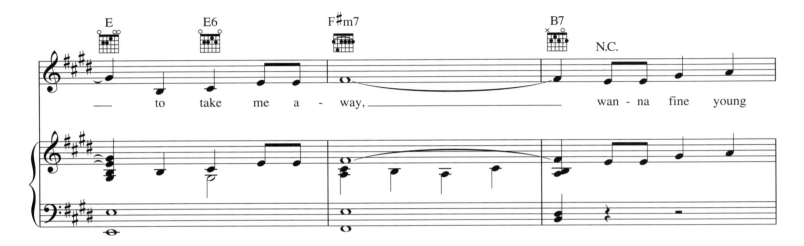

____ to take me a - way, ____ wan - na fine young

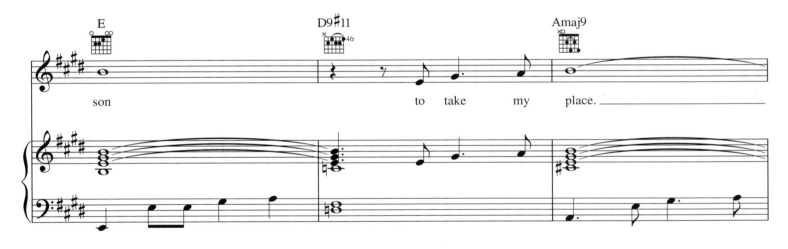

son to take my place. ____

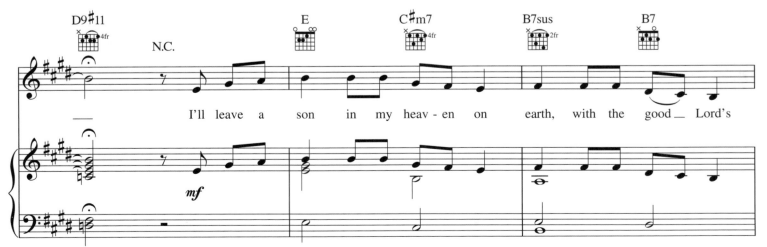

____ I'll leave a son in my heav - en on earth, with the good ____ Lord's

Grandioso

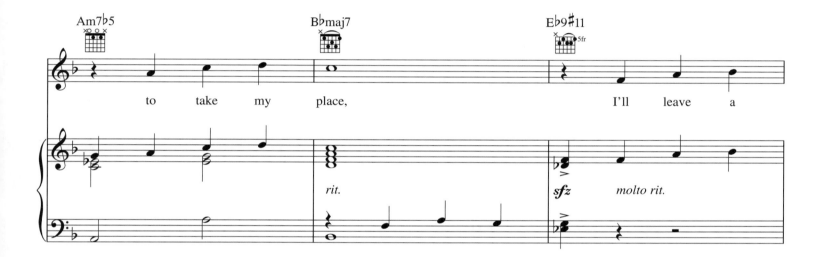

Extra Verses

Gonna build a heaven from a little hell.
Gonna build a heaven, and I know darn well,
With a fine young son to take my place
There'll be a sun in my heaven on earth
With the good Lord's grace.

Gonna build a mountain from a little hill.
Gonna build a mountain – least I hope I will.
Gonna build a mountain – gonna build it high.
I don't know how I'm gonna do it –
Only know I'm gonna try.

GYPSY IN MY SOUL

Words by MOE JAFFE and CLAY BOLAND
Music by CLAY BOLAND

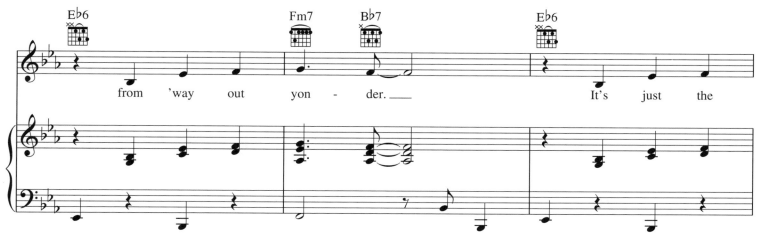

from 'way out yon - der. ___ It's just the

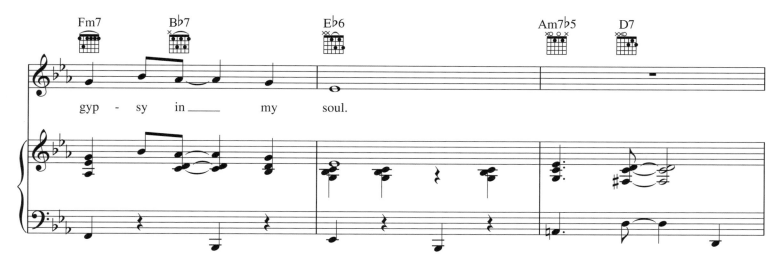

gyp - sy in ___ my soul.

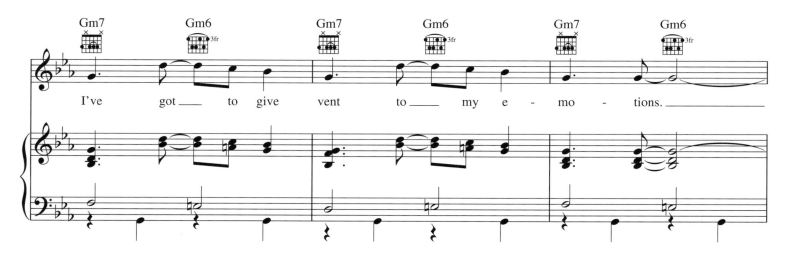

I've got ___ to give vent to ___ my e - mo - tions. ___

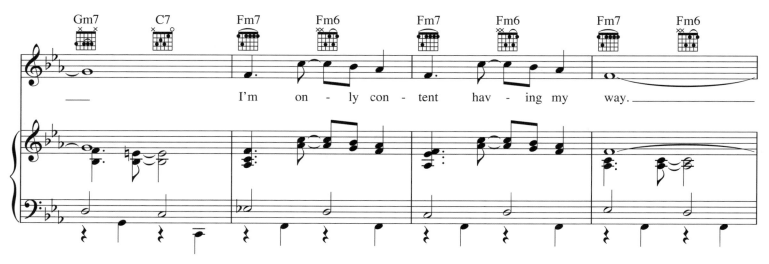

___ I'm on - ly con - tent hav - ing my way. ___

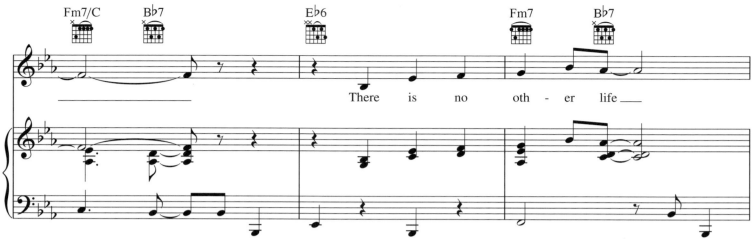

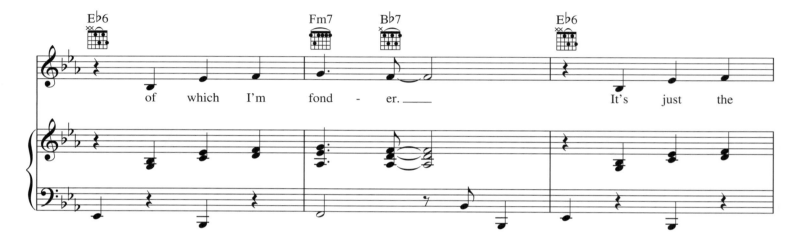

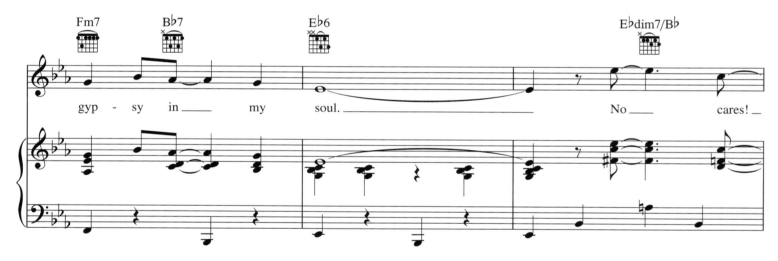

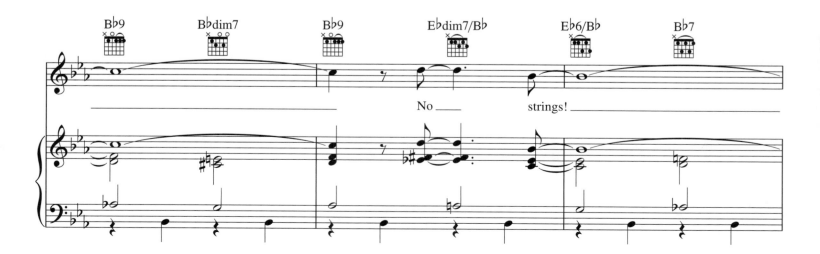

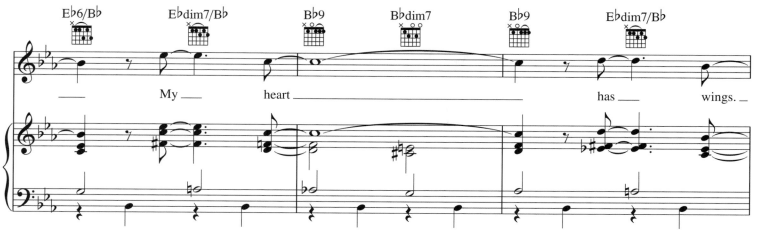

My ___ heart _____ has ___ wings. ___

_____ If I am fan - cy free, ___

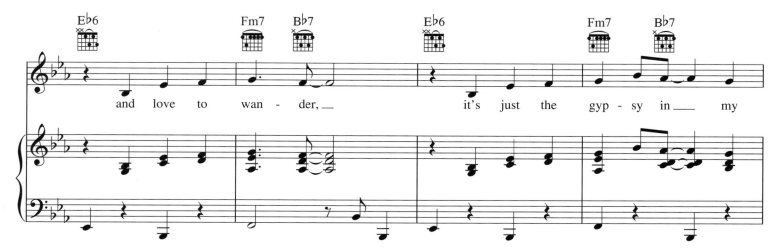

and love to wan - der, ___ it's just the gyp - sy in ___ my

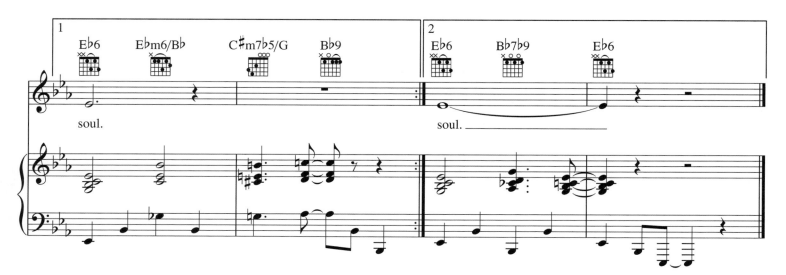

soul.   soul. _____

I GUESS I'LL HANG MY TEARS OUT TO DRY

Words by SAMMY CAHN
Music by JULE STYNE

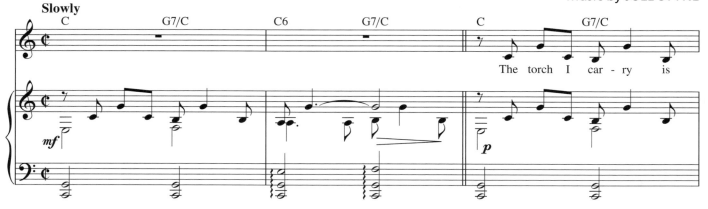

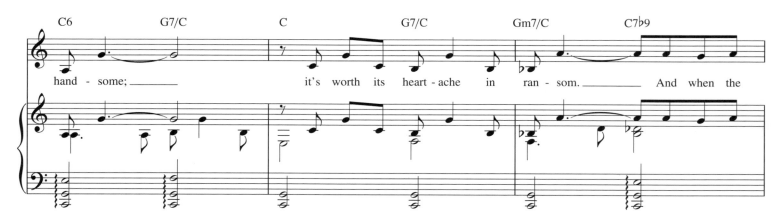

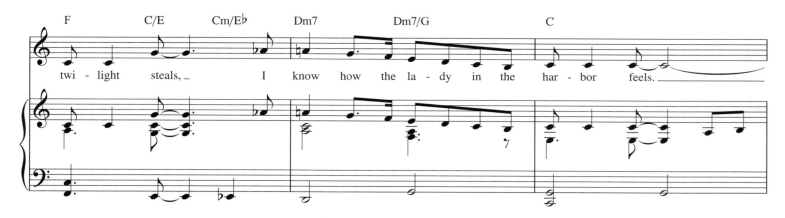

Guess I'll hang my tears out to dry. ____ Dry, lit-tle tear-drops,

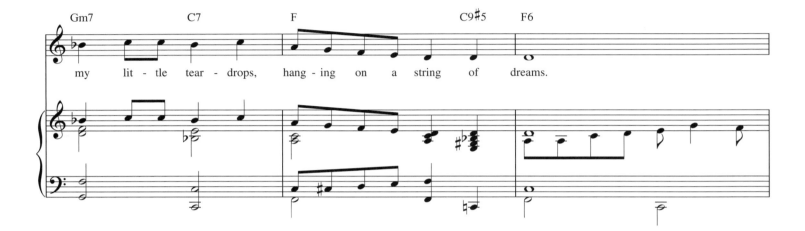

my lit-tle tear-drops, hang-ing on a string of dreams.

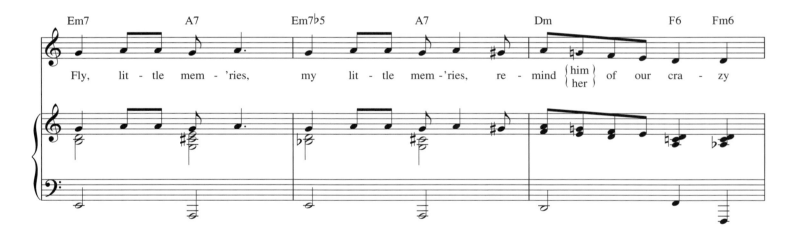

Fly, lit-tle mem-'ries, my lit-tle mem-'ries, re-mind {him}{her} of our cra-zy

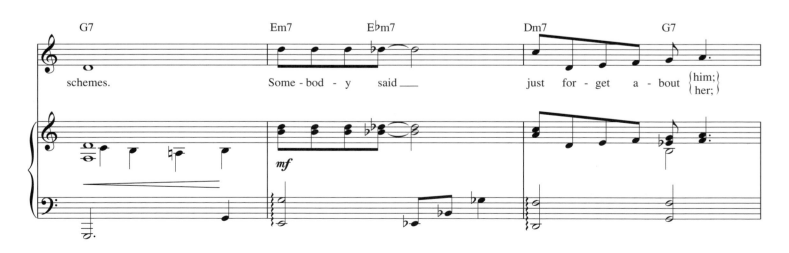

schemes. Some-bod-y said ____ just for-get a-bout {him;}{her;}

I gave that treat-ment a try. ____ Strange-ly e - nough, ____ I

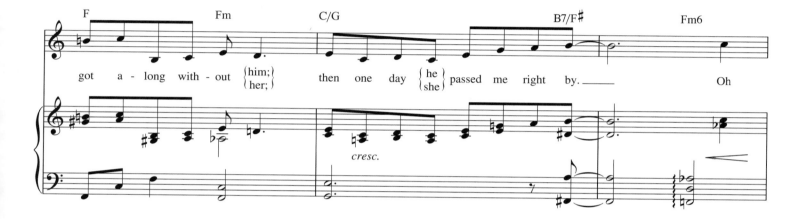

got a - long with - out {him; / her;} then one day {he / she} passed me right by. ____ Oh

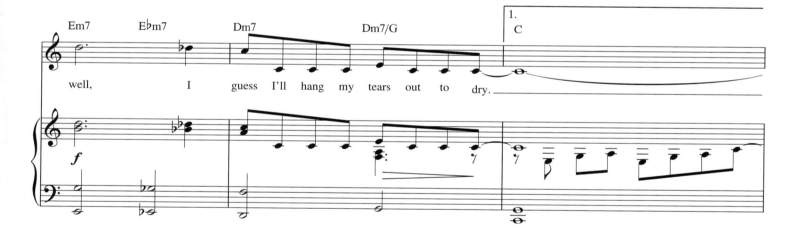

well, I guess I'll hang my tears out to dry. ____

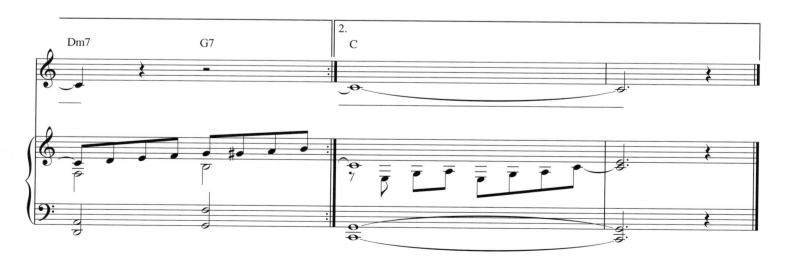

I'LL KNOW
from GUYS AND DOLLS

By FRANK LOESSER

I'M ALWAYS CHASING RAINBOWS

Words by JOSEPH McCARTHY
Music by HARRY CARROLL

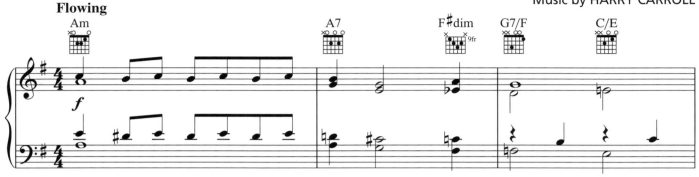

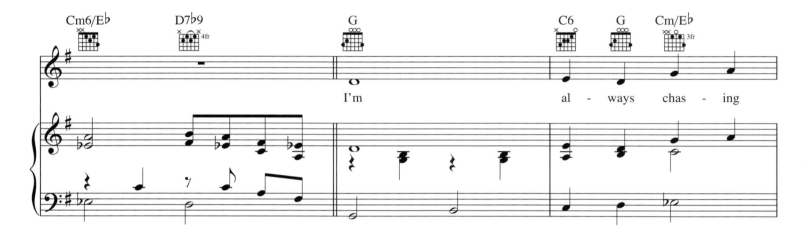

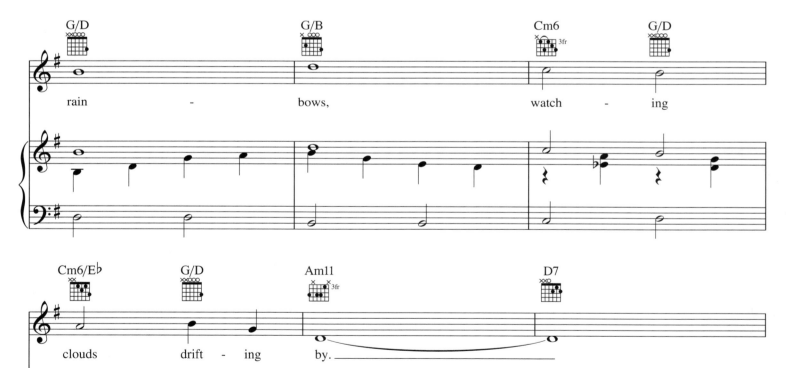

I'm al-ways chas-ing rain - bows, watch-ing

clouds drift-ing by. ____

My schemes are just like all my

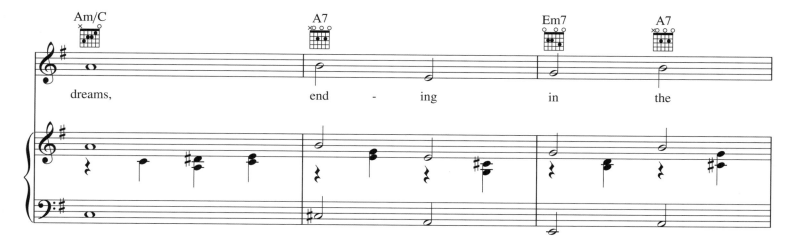

dreams, end - ing in the

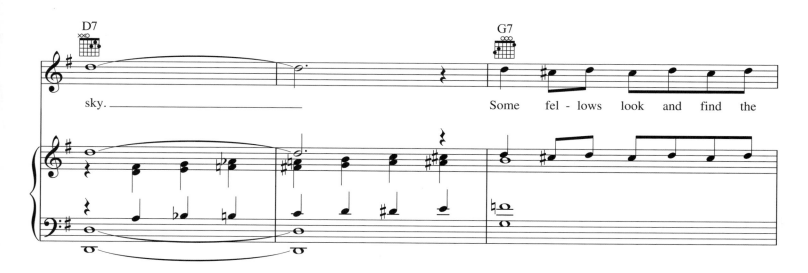

sky. _____ Some fel - lows look and find the

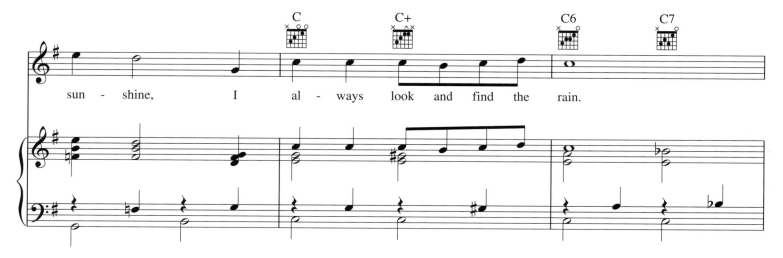

sun - shine, I al - ways look and find the rain.

Some fel - lows make a win - ning some - time, I nev - er e - ven make a

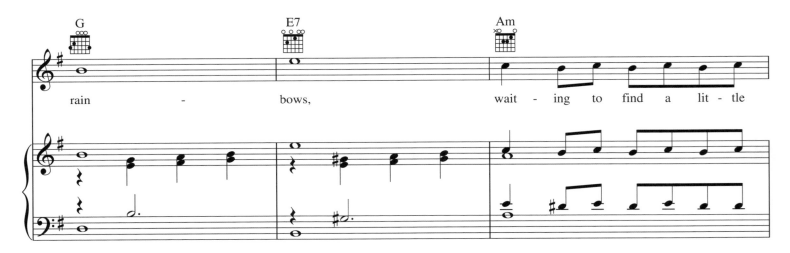

gain. Be - lieve me, I'm al - ways chas - ing

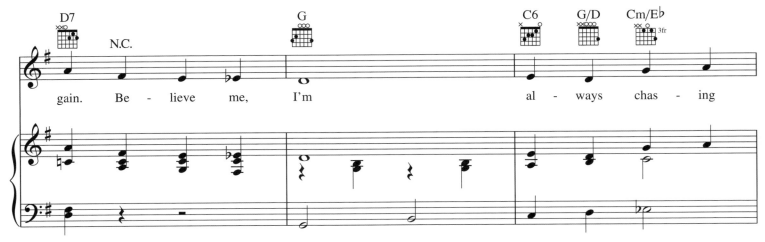

rain - bows, wait - ing to find a lit - tle

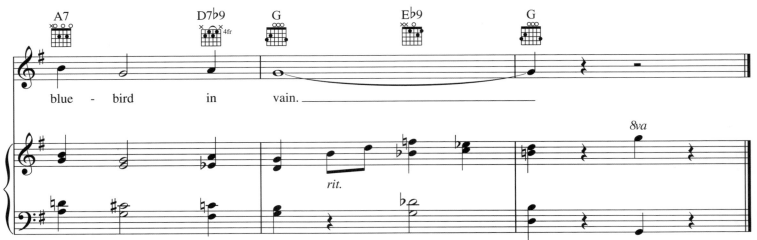

blue - bird in vain. _____

THE SHELTER OF YOUR ARMS

Words and Music by
JERRY SAMUELS

With conviction

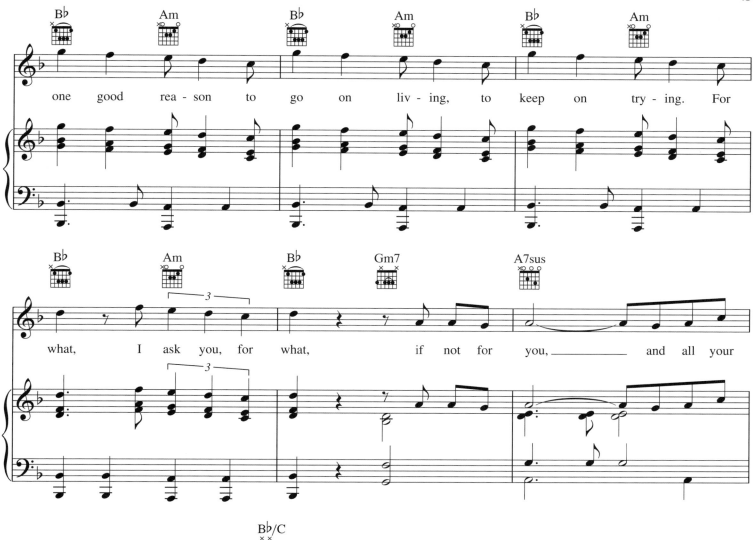

one good rea-son to go on liv-ing, to keep on try-ing. For

what, I ask you, for what, if not for you, _____ and all your

love, to see me through? _____

D.S. al Coda

When

CODA

all of my life, un-til the day I die. _____

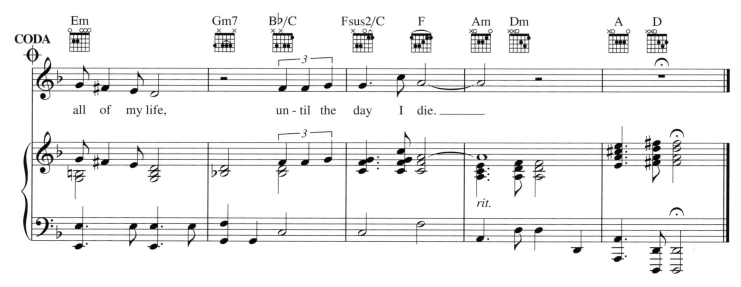

I'VE GOTTA BE ME

Music and Lyrics by
WALTER MARKS

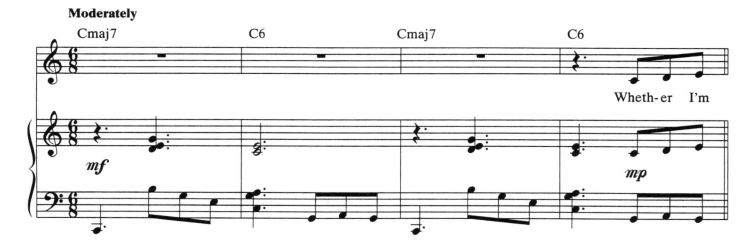

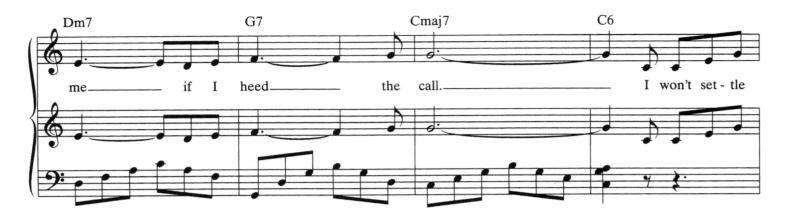

me_____ if I heed_____ the call._____ I won't set - tle

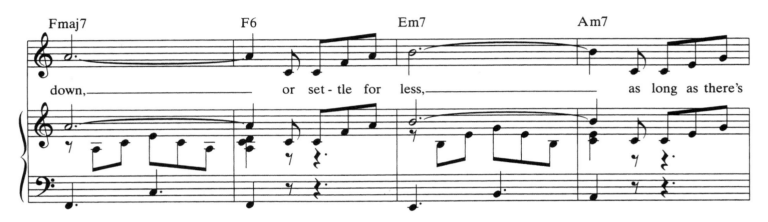

down,_____ or set - tle for less,_____ as long as there's

half a chance that I can have it all!_____ I'll go it a -

lone,_____ that's how it must be._____ I can't be

right for some-bod-y else if I'm not right for me!_____ I've got-ta be

free!_____ I've got-ta be free!_____ Dar-ing to

try to do it or die! I've got-ta be me!_____

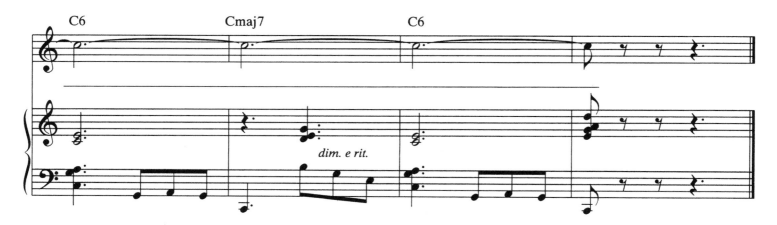

dim. e rit.

LET THERE BE LOVE

Lyric by IAN GRANT
Music by LIONEL RAND

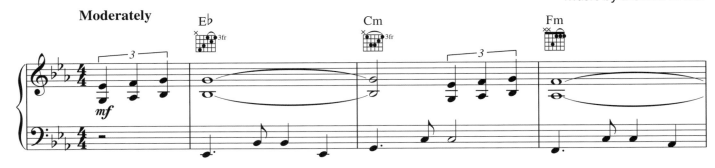

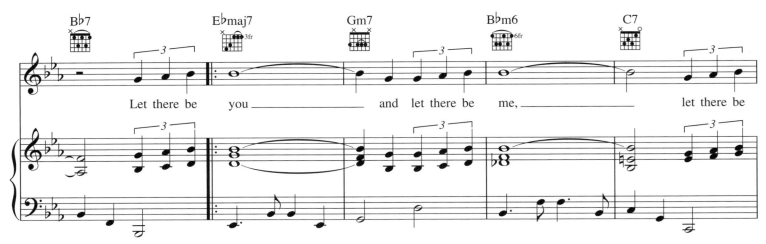

Let there be you _____ and let there be me, _____ let there be

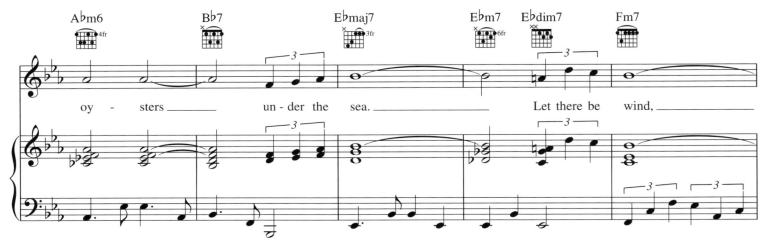

oy - sters _____ un - der the sea. _____ Let there be wind, _____

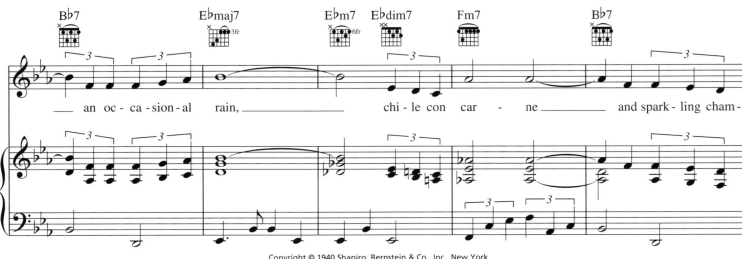

_____ an oc - ca - sion - al rain, _____ chi - le con car - ne _____ and spark - ling cham-

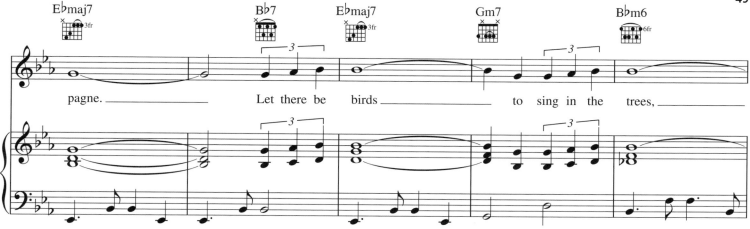

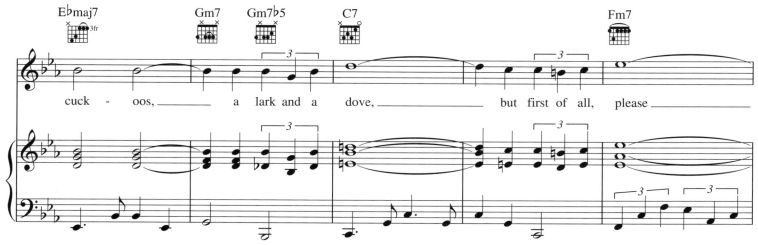

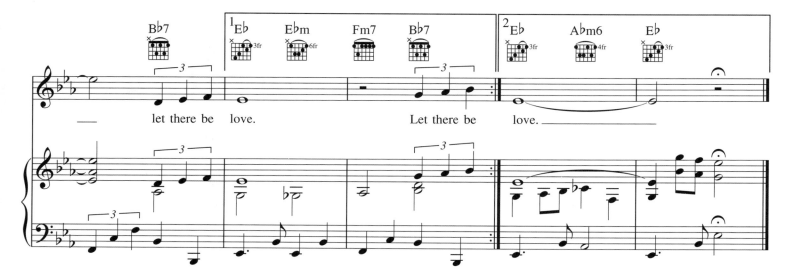

A LOT OF LIVIN' TO DO

from BYE BYE BIRDIE

Lyric by LEE ADAMS
Music by CHARLES STROUSE

With a steady growing drive

Refrain

There are {girls}{guys} just ripe for some kiss - in'___ And I

mean to kiss___ me a few! Oh, those

{girls}{guys} don't know___ what they're miss - in',___ I've

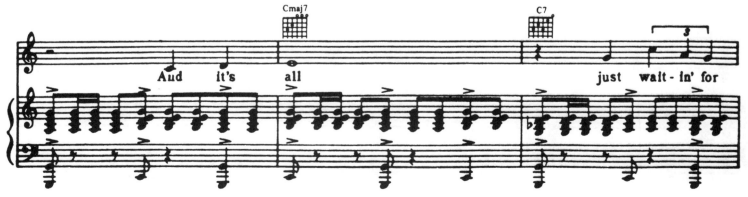

LOVE ME OR LEAVE ME

Lyrics by GUS KAHN
Music by WALTER DONALDSON

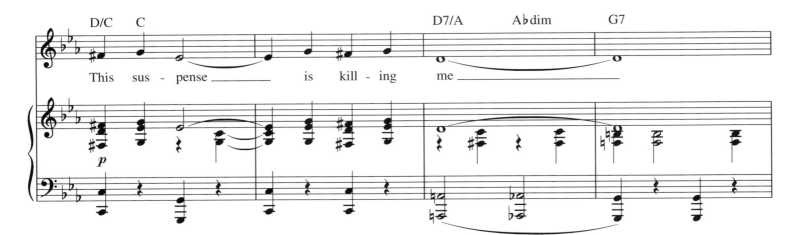

This sus- pense _____ is kill- ing me _____

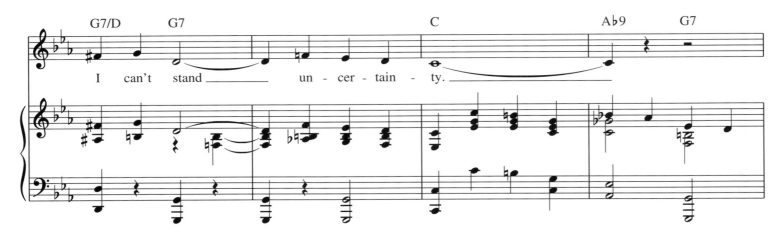

I can't stand _____ un- cer- tain- ty.

Tell me now _____ I've got to know _____

Wheth-er you want me ___ to stay or go. ___

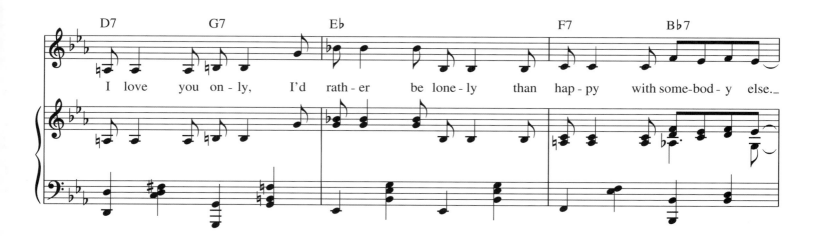

Love me or leave me and let me be lone-ly, You won't be-lieve me, and

I love you on-ly, I'd rath-er be lone-ly than hap-py with some-bod-y else. ___

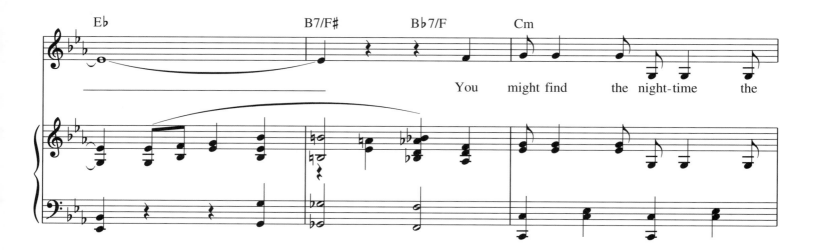

___ You might find the night-time the

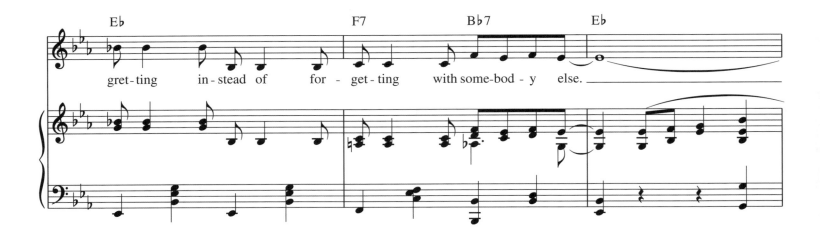

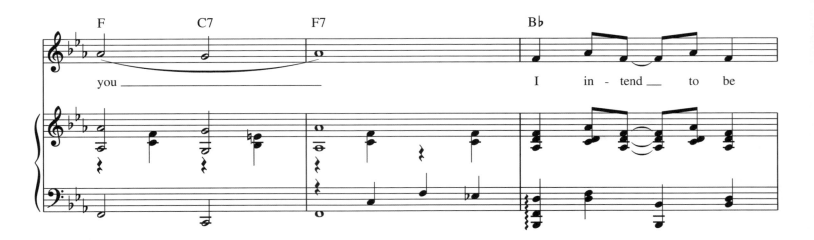

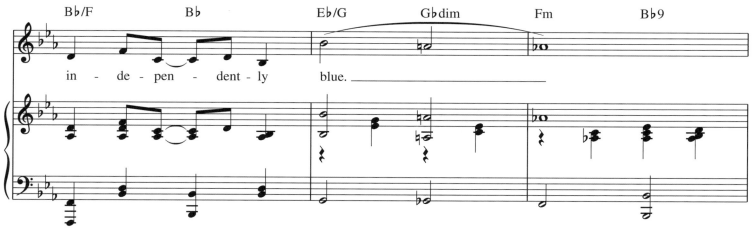

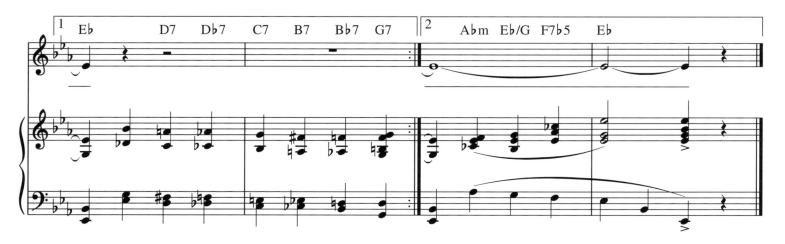

MR. BOJANGLES

Words and Music by
JERRY JEFF WALKER

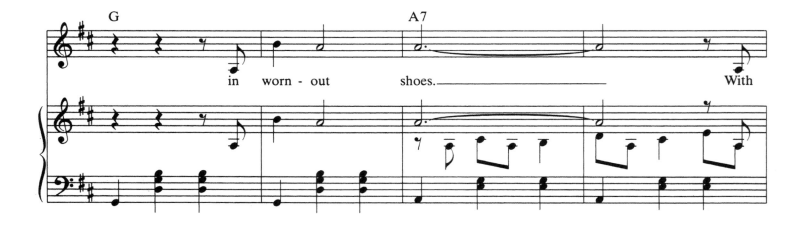

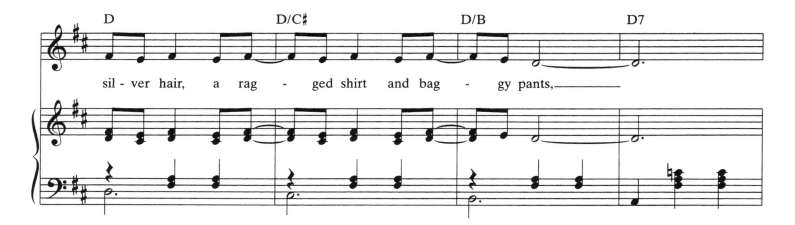

silver hair, a ragged shirt and baggy pants,

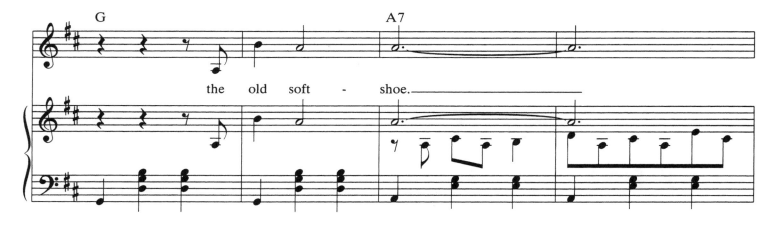

the old soft-shoe.

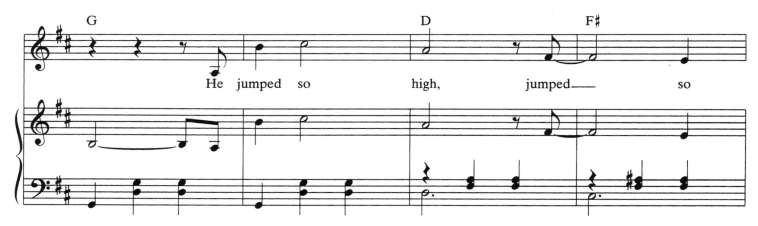

He jumped so high, jumped so

high, then he lightly touched down.

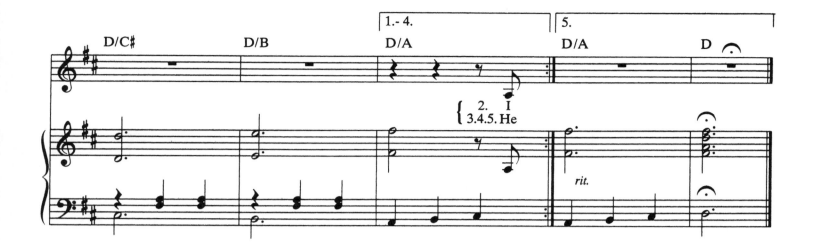

Additional Lyrics

2. I met him in a cell in New Orleans,
   I was down and out.
   He looked at me to be the eyes of age
   As he spoke right out.
   He talked of life, talked of life,
   He laughed, slapped his leg a step. *(To Chorus)*

3. He said his name, Bojangles, then he danced a lick
   Across the cell.
   He grabbed his pants, a better stance, oh he jumped up high,
   He clicked his heels.
   He let go a laugh, let go a laugh.
   Shook back his clothes all around. *(To Chorus)*

4. He danced for those at minstrel shows and county fairs
   Throughout the South.
   He spoke with tears of fifteen years how his dog and he
   Traveled about.
   His dog up and died, he up and died.
   After twenty years he still grieved. *(To Chorus)*

5. He said, "I dance now at every chance in honky-tonks
   For drinks and tips.
   But most of the time I spend behind these county bars."
   He said, "I drinks a bit."
   He shook his head and as he shook his head,
   I heard someone ask, please… *(To Chorus)*

PEOPLE TREE

Words and Music by LESLIE BRICUSSE
and ANTHONY NEWLEY

From the ap-ple comes the seed that grows in you and me.

From the seed comes the need to cre-ate an-oth-er tree. A tree that grows for ev-'ry man and

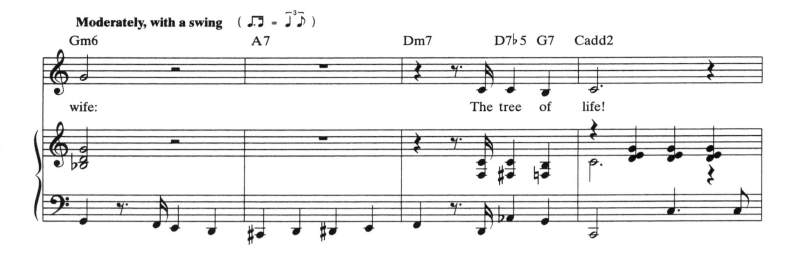

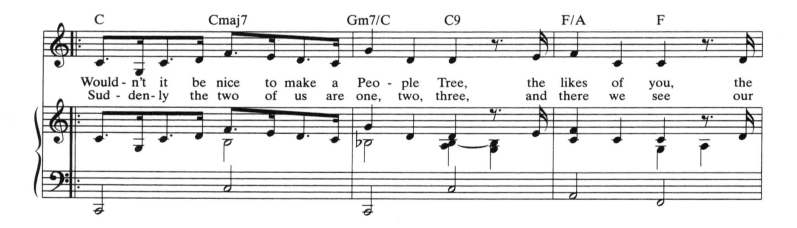

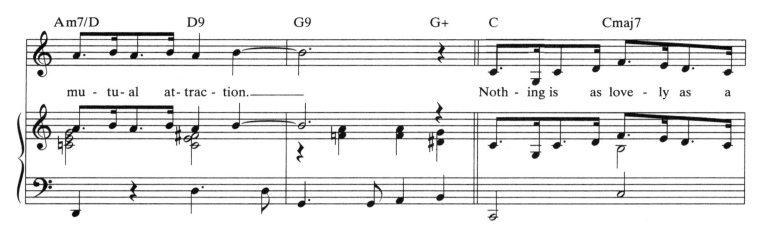

mu - tu - al at - trac - tion._____ Noth - ing is as love - ly as a

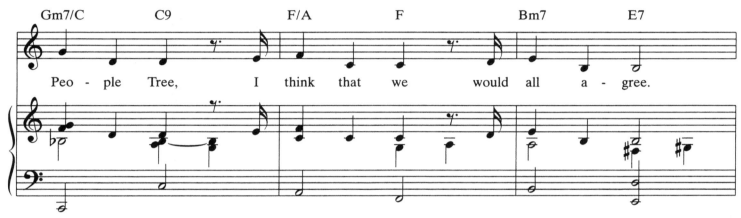

Peo - ple Tree, I think that we would all a - gree.

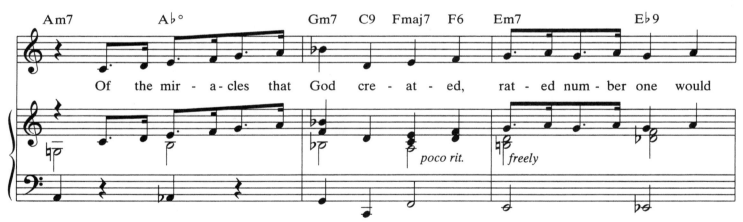

Of the mir - a - cles that God cre - at - ed, rat - ed num - ber one would

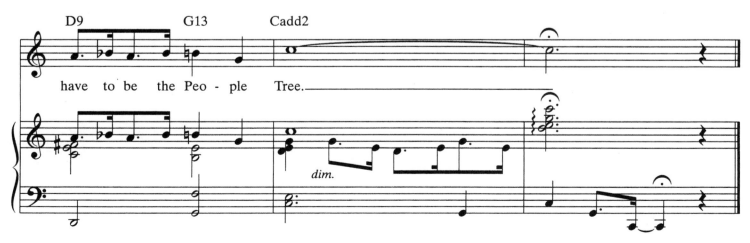

have to be the Peo - ple Tree._____

SMILE, DARN YA, SMILE

Words by CHARLES O'FLYNN and JACK MESKILL
Music by MAX RICH

Moderately

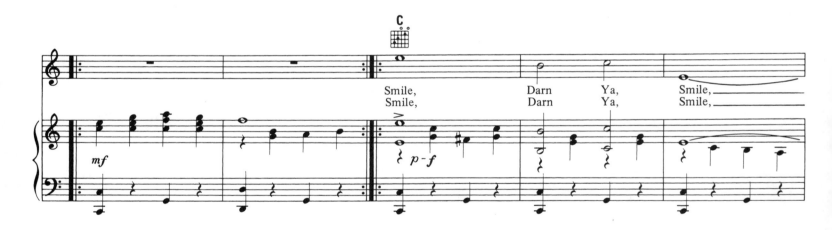

Smile,
Smile,
Darn Ya,
Darn
Smile,
Smile,

You know this old world is a great world af-ter all.
For there is noth-ing that you can-not o-ver-come.

SOMETHING'S GOTTA GIVE

Words and Music by
JOHNNY MERCER

THAT OLD BLACK MAGIC

from the Paramount Picture STAR SPANGLED RHYTHM

Words by JOHNNY MERCER
Music by HAROLD ARLEN

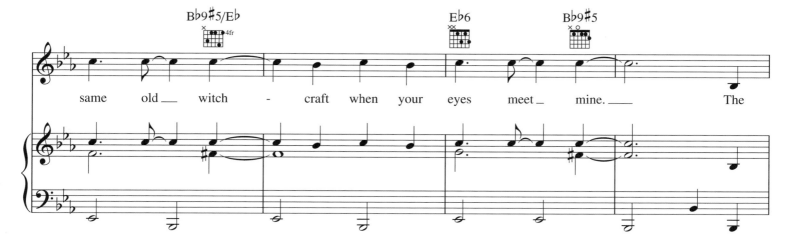

same old __ witch - craft when your eyes meet __ mine. __ The

same old __ tin - gle that I feel in - side, __ and

cresc. poco a poco

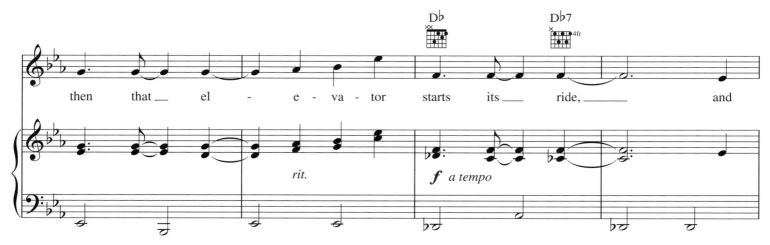

then that __ el - e - va - tor starts its __ ride, __ and

rit.   *f a tempo*

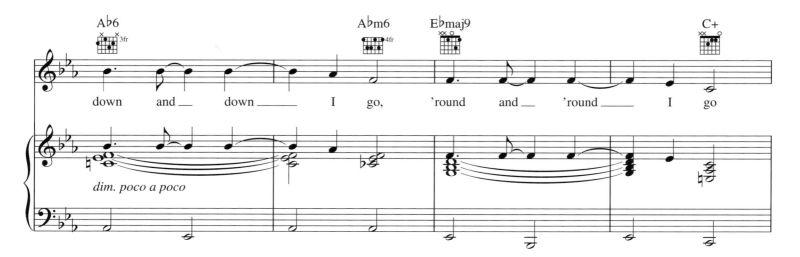

down and __ down __ I go, 'round and __ 'round __ I go

dim. poco a poco

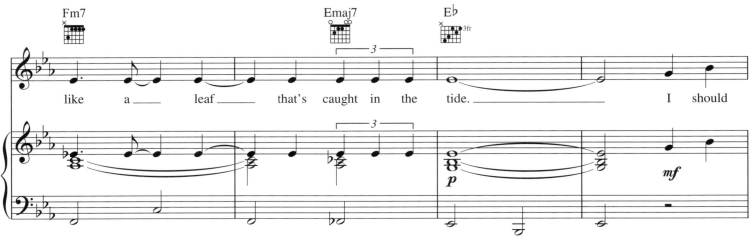

like a ___ leaf ___ that's caught in the tide. ___ I should

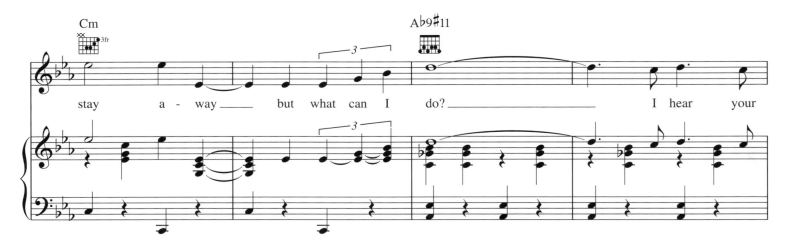

stay a-way ___ but what can I do? ___ I hear your

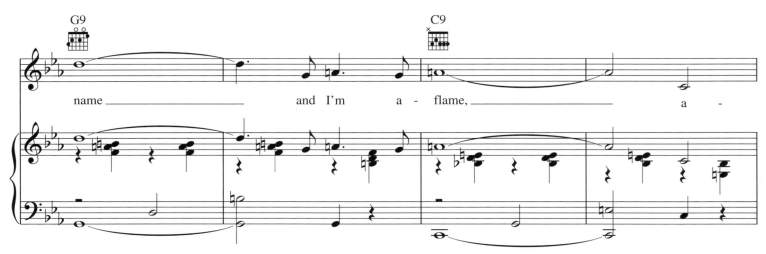

name ___ and I'm a-flame, ___ a-

flame with such ___ a burn-ing de-sire ___ that on-ly your

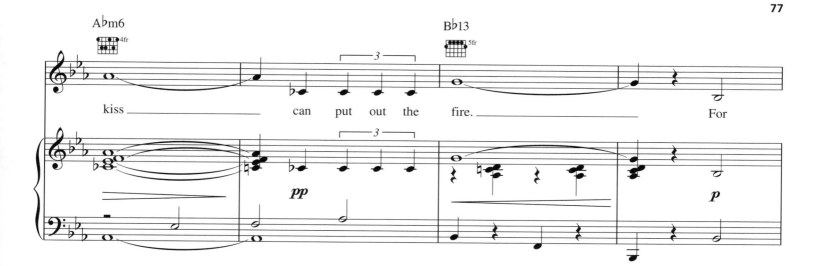

kiss _____ can put out the fire. _____ For

you're the ___ lov - er I have wait - ed ___ for, _____ the

mate that ___ fate _____ had me cre - at - ed ___ for, _____ and

ev - 'ry ___ time _____ your lips meet mine, _____ dar - ling,

THERE'S A SMALL HOTEL
from ON YOUR TOES

Words by LORENZ HART
Music by RICHARD RODGERS

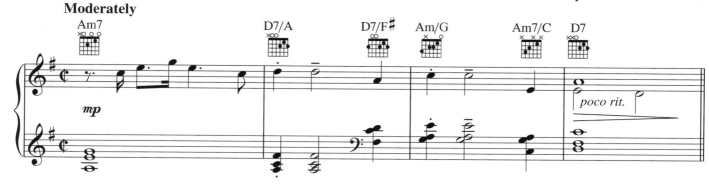

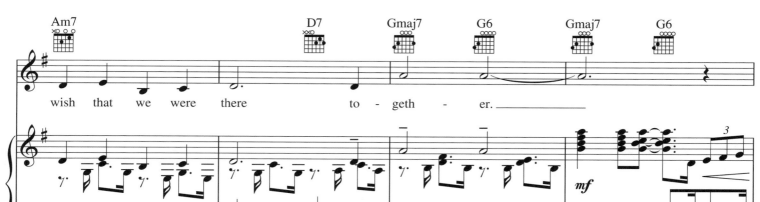

There's a small ho-tel With a wish-ing well; I

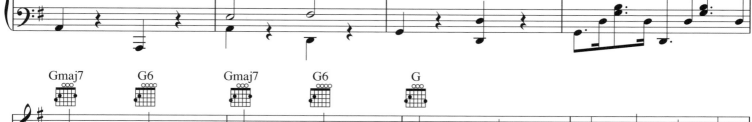

wish that we were there to-geth- er. _____

There's a brid-al suite; One room bright and neat, Com -

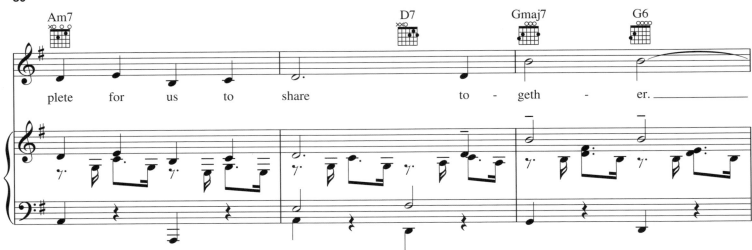

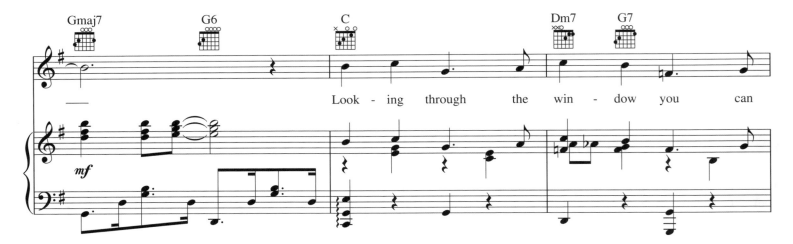

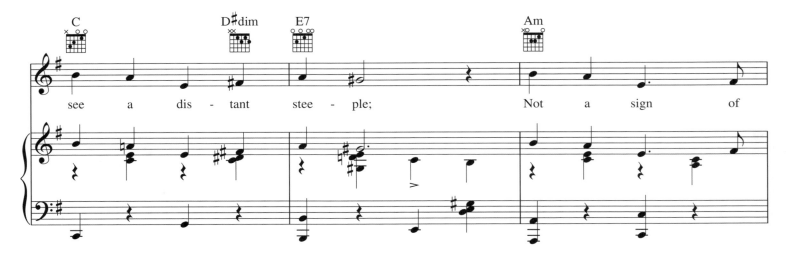

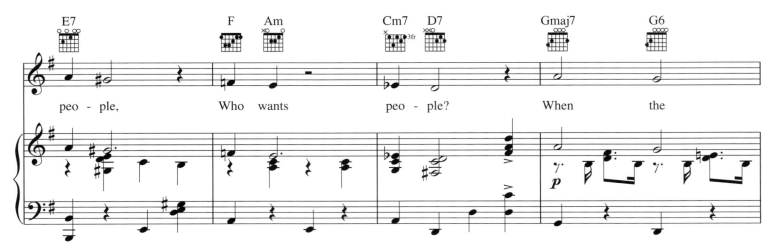

stee - ple bell says, "Good - night, sleep well," we'll

thank the small ho - tel to - geth - er.

tel. We'll creep in - to our lit - tle shell And we will

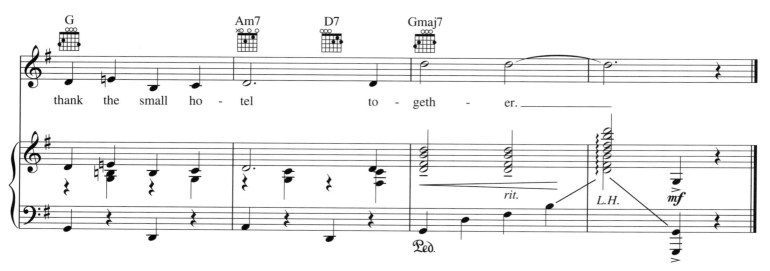

thank the small ho - tel to - geth - er.

TOO CLOSE FOR COMFORT

from the Musical MR. WONDERFUL

Words and Music by JERRY BOCK,
LARRY HOLOFCENER and GEORGE WEISS

now! _____ Be

now! _____

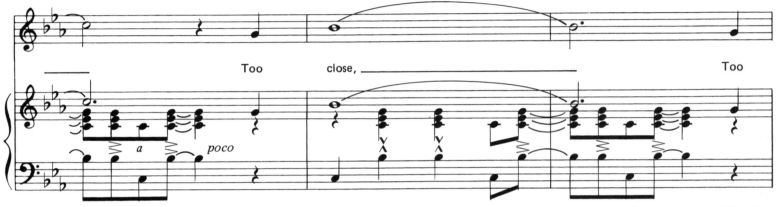

Too close, _____ Too

close. _____

{ 'She's / He's } much too _____ close for com - fort

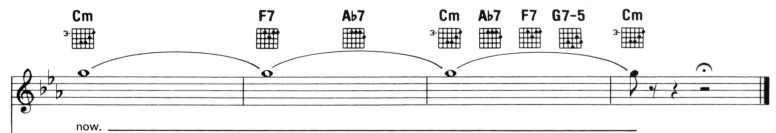

now. _____

WHAT KIND OF FOOL AM I?

from the Musical Production STOP THE WORLD–I WANT TO GET OFF

Words and Music by LESLIE BRICUSSE
and ANTHONY NEWLEY

Moderately slow

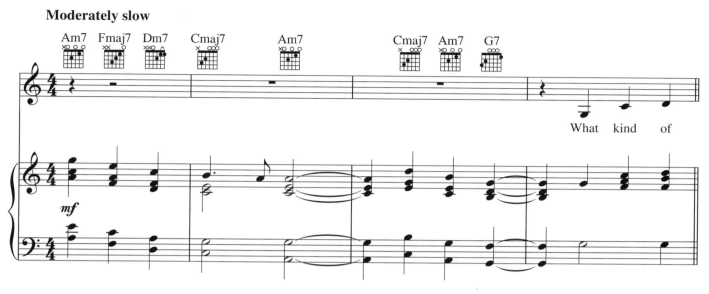

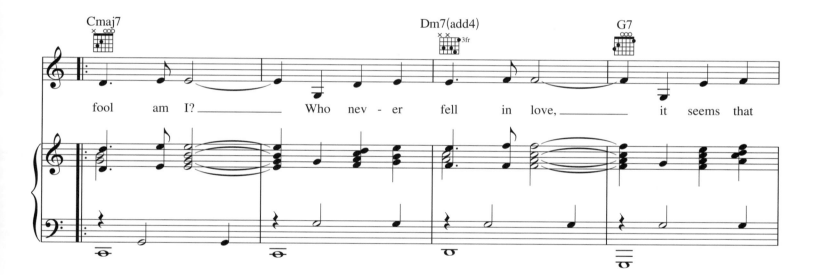

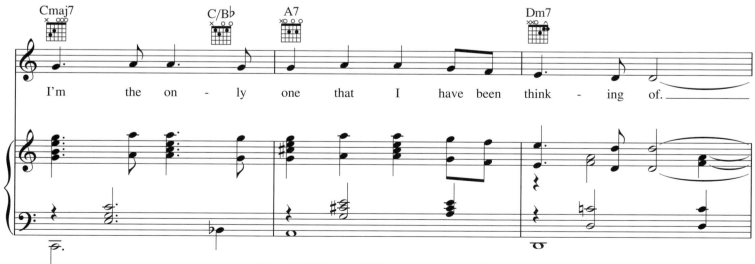

YES I CAN

Words and Music by LEE ADAMS
and CHARLES STROUSE

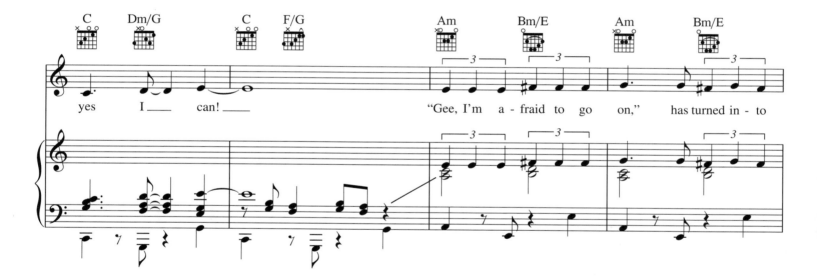

yes _____ I _____

can! _____

Yes I ___ can! ___ Sud-den-ly, yes I ___ can! ___

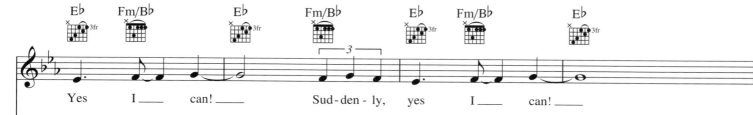

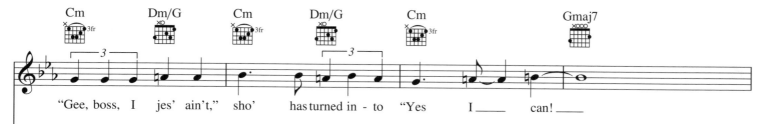

"Gee, boss, I jes' ain't," sho' has turned in-to "Yes I ___ can! ___

I have just found the key! Hey, door, swing wide for me.

I was just born to-day, I can go all the way,

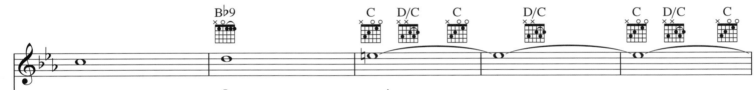

yes I can!

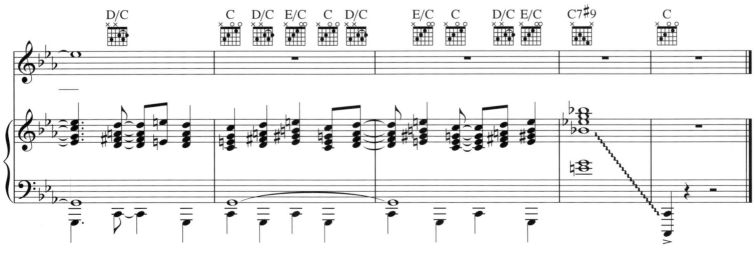